Breaking Design

Poetry by

Connie Larson Miller

PBL Limited
Ottumwa Iowa

Copyright 2008 by Connie Larson Miller

Cover design copyright 2008 by Michael W. Lemberger
Cover art, The Cursy of the Broken Vase, copyright 2008 by Connie Larson Miller

Illustrations copyright 2008 by Connie Larson Miller

10 9 8 7 6 5 4 3 2 1

ISBN   1-892689-57-X
ISBN 13: 978-1-892689-57-3

Printed in the United States of America

Do You Remember Me?, first published in *Eclipsed Moon Coins*. **Abandoned Homestead Protected by Farm Bureau,** first published in *Eclipsed Moon Coins*. **May Day**, first published in *Lyrical Iowa*. **Just Things**, first published in *Eclipsed Moon Coins*. **Albert**, first published in *The Dryland Fish*. **Constructing A Paper Chain at the Crisis Center**, first published in *Lyrical Iowa*. **Eating Bitter Bread**, first published in the Crisis Center newsletter. **Newsreel,** first published in *Lyrical Iowa*. **Albert,** first published in *Lyrical Iowa*. **The Women At the Well**, first published in *Lyrical Iowa*. **Loopholes**, first published in *Lyrical Iowa*. **Milkweed Pods**, first published in *The Dryland Fish*. **Driving Good Gifts into Hiding**, first published in *Leaves by Night, Flowers by Day*. **Still Life with Missing Dog**, first published by *Lyrical Iowa*. **The Breakfast Nooks Story** was first published in *Iowa Heritage* magazine, 2002.

The Curtsy of the Broken Vase, art by Connie Larson Miller, was sold at the Sister Kenney Foundation in Abbott Hospitals, Minneapolis, Minn. **Green Tomatoes in Still Life,** art by Connie Larson Miller, is reproduced courtesy of Wanda and Richard Collett.

All rights reserved. Except for brief passages quoted in any review, the reproduction or utilization of this work in whole or in part, in any form or by any electronic, mechanical, or other means, now known or hereinafter invented, including xerography, photocopying and recording, or in any information storage and retrieval system, is forbidden without the express permission of the publisher. For permission contact:
    Rights Editor
    PBL Limited
    P.O. Box 935
    Ottumwa IA 52501-0935
    www.pbllimited.com

Copies of this book are available from PBL Limited. See page 74 for details on ordering by mail, or visit our website at www.pbllimited.com for more information.

For

Matthew, Melissa, and Chase

Breaking Design

"There's a tree that grows in Brooklyn.
Some people call it the Tree of Heaven.
No matter where the seed falls, it makes a tree
which struggles to reach the sky.
It grows lushly. Survives without sun, water,
seemingly without earth. It would be considered
beautiful except that there are too many of it."

-- Betty Smith
A Tree Grows in Brooklyn

Connie Larson Miller

This book is dedicated . . .

. . . To the teachers, counselors, and women's shelters who encourage children and women to express themselves. We praise you and give thanks for your gifts.

. . . To my family for second chances, I praise God.

. . . To women and children everywhere who endure to have character and then hope and faith, this is for you. Wherever you are, don't give up the pursuit of your peace. I am so grateful our lives have crossed; you have blessed my life.

Special thanks to Diane, Chet, Janet, and Susie. To Gretchen and Marg for listening. To Linda, who has been at my computer side these many years. To Leigh and Michael for the opportunity to work with them. To my writing groups, who have been there for me. To VSA Arts Iowa, a group of artists who encourage Arts, Disability and Culture. To American Association of University Women, Iowa Pen Women, and the Iowa Poetry Association.

--Connie Larson Miller

Table of Contents

Breaking Design   8
Fat Tuesday   10
To the Children of Father Flanagan's Boys and Girls Home   11
And the Rains Came   12
Do You Remember Me?   15
Botulism   16
May Day   17
First Entry in a Writing Contest   18
"Goin' to Kansas City" To the "Waltz of the Flowers"   20
Any Good Swede Knows How to Make White Sauce   21
Flip Flops   23
Acceleration   23
Pink Celluloid Christmas on Melrose Place   24
Behind Huston Field   25
Hello My Name is _____.   26
Abandoned Homestead Protected by Farm Bureau   27
The Advocate   28
Magical Powers   30
Just Things   32
Catherine   32
Still Life with Missing Dog   33
Prairie Chicken   34
At First She Only Flew When No One Looked   36
Albert   37
Milkweed Pods   38
Mama's Macaroni's Special Sauce   39
On the Way to Minnesota   40
Rich Vein   41
Baby With An Old Soul   42
Shaylee   43
May 7, 1945   45

Connie Larson Miller

Cornflower Blue   46
The Year's Curve   47
The December Earth Speaks   48
Eating Bitter Bread   50
Newsreel   51
The Women at the Well   52
Planing the Board   53
The Road That Brought Us Here   54
Jewelry Store Sky   55
XX Chromosome   56
The Hard Part   57
Constructing a Paper Chain at the Crisis Center   58
Loop Holes   59
Paisley Ghost Sighting II   60
Waiting for an Oil Change   61
At the Chat and Chew on Main   62
The Breakfast Nook Story   64
Lady with a Lathe   67
Smug Sydney   68
Driving Good Gifts into Hiding   68
Cardinal   69
Sunday is In Me Now   70
Night-Time Blessings   71
Closing   72

Breaking Design

The recess bell pierces
my syncopated day.
I drop my art supply box.
Your classmates stop
to question who is the stranger?
Cautiously you enter the room,
I comment on the sponge painted animals
of your tee shirt, I carefully
ignore the stain and rip.
Inching a bit closer, your eyes
peek up from the floor,
through out-grown hair stubble.
Teaching you to draw pattern with oil pastel,
your teacher tells me you may talk about fire.
Sure enough you decorate with fire,
and your half-brother makes a firefly.
"What do I know about pattern?" I wonder.
Do I say things were difficult for me,
it was hard work?
Do I tell you your life
isn't carved in stone?

You raise your hand, call me by name,
ask me how to spell butterfly?
And write I-like-my-butterfly.
Let me paste wings on you!
You smile.
I'm addicted.

And on the way home the words
of my late Father are ringing
in my ears, about the joys of creativity.
He'd say "You can't put a price on that."
I'm comforted by those words
momentarily. Later, I obsess on how
two seven year old boys
will establish trust.

Years pass. I realize
I was the one who
was unable to trust.

Breaking Design

Fat Tuesday

We huddle together in the basement of the coliseum
Whispering well wishes for the other one
before the coronation of the queen.
Raven hair contrasting with your white tulle gown.
Fire and ice lipstick sculpting
your hundred-watt smile
You tell me you learned to brush your teeth
to fill the boredom.

Your pre-med student prince
has driven all night from a Bible college
in Indiana to escort you.

The summer after graduation
you wait on me at Williams Dairy.
Pale lips faintly mention
you read Willa Cather and Pearl S. Buck.
He has selected these for you.

Karen caught the bouquet at your wedding.
We were the only two the bridegroom trusted.
The last time we meet at spring break
you tell me you'll be learning to play bridge
as that's what doctors' wives do.
Dull eyes void of the radiance
they once held when you appeared
at the orphanage in seventh grade.

Your foster mother tells me
she wishes she knew what happened
to you and your children after the divorce,
as I rock my three children to hymns
that comfort me and cry for the poison
that engulfed us.

As Always, same best wishes.
Always Mardi-Gras, Fat Tuesday.

Connie Larson Miller

To the Children
of Father Flanagan's Boys and Girls Home

As I look over my mail spread out over the kitchen table,
I decide to write to you this evening while I was still able.
I wrote and rewrote, past dark, into night
while the moon, stars and then sun shone their festive light.
For you see my favorite time of year is nearing
and my mailbox was full of holiday pleas, and cheering.
Catalogues for toy trains and ornaments that glisten
plus requests from Missions and Boys Town to listen.
But my heart belongs to a five year old boy
who wanted to buy me a mansion instead of a toy.
This little boy, now grown, whose name is Chase,
was raised by his Father far from this meager place.

Yes, I was one of those Mothers who wasn't strong enough, you see,
to raise children as loving and lively as these three.

Breaking Design

And the Rains Came

In July I could smell the mold
through the TV, glancing at pictures
of Grand Rapids. Rubbing against
the picture tube, the scum would stay
liked a crushed, imaginary waterline
on my clothes. This year it wasn't us.

In '93 it was me watching the 75-year-old
oak slowly teeter, then give way
to rushing current, just over the highway
on Rabbit Run. It fell gracefully
as if it was taking its final bow
to a standing ovation.

I wake to sirens, an announcer
blaring "Prepare to evacuate."
A vacuum cleaner whirls in my stomach
as I suck up baby pictures into my arms,
adding the toy roller coaster
I bought to represent my life
for what I thought to be
my next ride out of hills and valleys.

One by one mobile homes move
out of the park as the panic spreads.
I glue myself to the radio and TV
for news of Red Rock Dam.

Connie Larson Miller

A taxi pulls up outside, lets out Wally,
who stumbles toward the door,
a gray shadow of a former self.
He wants to reminisce about high school *daze*.
He sits smoking cigarettes he borrows
from me, completely surrounded by chairs
on top of tables, immune. When
I am short with him, I feel as bad
as if I'd been wiped out by the flood.

"I thought maybe you'd be filling sandbags today?" I hint.
"No I just thought I'd look you up."
"I'm just to busy too visit today, Wally," I say.

"Well, I'll go," and from the porch
he calls back over his shoulder, "I love you."
You know, he does, but right now I'm the last card
played in his losing game of solitaire.

He sees me as the Queen of Hearts
in a life he doesn't understand.
I bargained for an Ace of Spades,
many times myself, Wally.
Life is so much brighter
when you can see both sides,
and I ever so gently wish that for you.

Raindrops start to pound on my tin roof
as I wipe the rust from my cheek.

Breaking Design

Connie Larson Miller

Do You Remember Me?

I was the one in the last pew at church,
feeling unchurched in church,
astounding you by the rules I broke.
I felt Christ's death that Good Friday,
the silence moving off into years.
I remember the one particular Marlboro
I smoked in the church basement
like it was the only one I'd ever smoked in my life.
It was before removing the black veil from the altar.
I gave you the finger that morning after
you told me you liked married women
better than untrained ones.
The bittersweet taste of Easter.

Once again Christ is risen,
but did he die for my sins.
You say I'm afraid to love,
no mention of the greatest love of all.
You, our guru -- who no one can escape.
Trying, I sheepishly thank you for all you had done.
Your comment: "You are welcome to the human race."
Do you remember me?

Twenty years later
I travel to a friend's wedding you officiate.
I sat on the aisle that day.
Is it a memory of a twisted mind
or was it professional incompetence?
You talked of the flowers at the arboretum,
how each one, like humans, is created differently,
and about molecules and how they attract.
Molecules also oppose.
Considering myself someone who has a voice still,
I turned my head when you called my name.
You said I'd talk again.
Is that what you were afraid of all along?

Botulism

In my Grandmother's hoosier
tears are stored in jars.
Sterilized,
placed in cold pack,

they were saved
by my Grandmother's
shame at giving birth
six months after her wedding.

Her eldest child
chokes tears back for fifty years
in a mental institution. All trauma
stored, shackled, and restrained.

My mother tightens the lids on the jars,
afraid that knowledge of scar
might escape. Her Jacqueline Kennedy
grief holds everything in place.

But the jar lids bulge,
and Wednesday after Wednesday
on my drive home from work,
I jam on the brakes. Post Traumatic
Stress splinters glass.

May Day

Woven clover chains in your sunlit hair.
The three of you dancing
on a blanket of spring green grass
as dots of dandelions and violets
curtsy and bow.

I want to return to the creek once more,
to hear water babbling
over flat rocks and try to walk across
steep meadow pastures beyond.

As I come to the wooden gate
and show you my childhood country,
I want to take you to the barn loft
in search of newborn kittens,
nested in a Monet haystack,
and hear the stomp of horses' hooves
as they swish their tails at flies.

And if you close your eyes,
you too can be Kings and Queens
sitting in a wagon of corn
throwing gold to the peasant pigs.

Breaking Design

First Entry in a Writing Contest

My first jingle was written at the age of eight for Cheerios,
borrowed straight out of the Sunday funnies --
an advertisement for another cereal.
Laboring over the entry, I mailed it
with a five cent stamp at the corner mailbox
and forgot about it.

My mother announced to me
a few months later
I had received a letter form the LONE RANGER.
Elated, I tore open the letter and read:
"Congratulations! You are the winner of
the Cheerios Lone Ranger
Hollywood screen test contest."
Dancing and screaming for joy
around the dining room table, shrieking,
"I'm going to be a movie star in Hollywood."
My Mother suggested I read the whole letter,
continuing, "Your prize is
a complete Lone Ranger outfit. . ."

I recall the snapshot --
standing in front of the fireplace
pearl-handled six-guns drawn
from gem-studded black and white holsters.
My blond hair hanging to my shoulders,
under the cowboy hat onto the embroidery,
with matching black jeans trimmed with white piping.
As I lean on one cowboy boot,
the other boot with a bored right angle,
my mouth's turned down at the corners,
staring out the window, disinterestedly.

Years later my boys enjoyed the outfit and
it was thrown about the toy box until it vanished.

The letter was placed in a childhood scrapbook
which I tossed out after my divorce,
wanting to cleanse myself of the past.
Now every time my children say,
"Guess what we found at Dad's," I light up.
How sweet, he resurrected my scrapbook!

No such luck.
So now one of the reasons I write
is to recall a silo of nostalgia.
However, I was destined to write
at a young age
when I wrote:

CHEERIOS ARE DANDY
THEY TASTE LIKE CANDY

"Goin' to Kansas City" to the "Waltz of the Flowers"

We eight couples fast step
in the basement of an Arthur Murray
instructor's home. Mediterranean
scarlet sofa and thick dark-stained tables
with square brads at one end of the room,
then a specially installed ballroom dance floor
at the other end. We childless couples yawn
as we try to put bump in the rumba.

Years later, as a single
great lady of society that I am,
I corner a guy with a fifties ducktail
leaning on the bar at the Wild Rose and
ask him to take ballroom dancing
with me in a church basement.
He said he couldn't because
"Jesus wouldn't like it if I danced
in the church." Then he appears *readyalert*
on my porch Sunday morning with a can
of "Bud" in his hand.

So now I've danced to the music
of "Goin' to Kansas City"
and come back to Iowa family roots.
I've learned to record the growth of a garden plot.
Not to fight or snuff out a fire,
of the tempest surprise of a naked-lady lily stalk.
I circle the rim of a violet teacup --
dance as a silk scarf scatters sunlight,
humming the "Waltz of the Flowers."

Connie Larson Miller

Any Good Swede Knows How to Make White Sauce

"When it rains soup, the poor man has no spoon."
-- Old Swedish Proverb

Thin White Sauce
1 T. butter
1 T. flour
¼ t. salt
1/8 t. pepper
1 cup of milk

Heat butter in sauce pan over low heat until melted.
Blend in flour, salt and pepper. Cook over low heat,
stirring constantly, until smooth and bubbly;
remove from heat. Stir in milk. Heat to boiling,
stirring constantly. Boil and stir 1 minute.

Grandma Bertha used white sauce for everything--
as a base for the yummiest macaroni and cheese
to the smelliest creamed lutfisk.
To be a good Swede you ate
white food: creamed herring, ostkaka,
cucumber salad, potatoes in cream,
Swedish meatballs in sauce.
Nothing like a little white sauce to cover things up.

Then there was my college sorority.
The honor roll students were treated
to filet mignon. I usually sat
at the white table where the lower
grade points sat, served pasta and potatoes.
I, being of Swedish heritage, had been
prepared for the destiny.

Breaking Design

Connie Larson Miller

Flip Flops

Purple and turquoise
flip-flops prance a cha cha
with a battered flower.

Acceleration

A punch, caught off guard like a stolen basketball.
A fall, I trip on your vocabulary which I don't understand.
A bounce, be brave, be cool, he'll go away if ignored.

I try to flee from your ways of expressing manhood.
Drawing from the mixmaster of my mind, five hundred miles away.
Trying to be free, to fast forward myself through the words
that persist as fresh as the moment you spoke them a decade ago,
I push on the pedal to accelerate a new day.
The harder I try, the more you splatter my windshield
with grey globs of snow, slush, and dirt.

Reminding me you're more
than years,
miles,
and time,
can remove.

Breaking Design

Pink Celluloid Christmas on Melrose Place
For Charlotte

We kindred matrons call ourselves pillars of the porch,
follow sunflower-fed children to a L.A. beige beach.
Milestones ago, we wouldn't stop,
not for a humming motor gliding
on thin balsa wings, among damp seaweed
now trailing from our scarecrow arms.

We wrangle wineglasses on each occasion
over which newborn started the crying first
that baptismal Sunday long ago.

We glance sideways at the couple
next to us at the outdoor lunch on Melrose Place.
Purple spiked hair to match faux fur,
spider webs tattooed on her elbows.
Consider our luck.

Time pumped the calliope
through Holly Hobbie birthdays,
black arm-banded beer drinking songs,
and we wonder what happened
to the game of Clue.

The twin wedding summer
we deck out in threat
of flame-red sequined, slit gown
for first row pew perching,
and delight as they squirm at the possibility.

Once again this pink celluloid Christmas
our cross-stitched aprons
pull together silver-haired years,
stretch across reminiscing decades.

Connie Larson Miller

Behind Huston Field

Behind Huston Field there is a footbridge
over Kettle Creek. There, Janet
and Sharon and I smoked
our first cigarette which tasted like
they had been in the family for generations.
We pass the stub back and forth, choking
over our new experience.

The L & Ms lay in a carton
in the kitchen drawer,
two hundred soldiers
all lined up waiting to attack,
too available for our itchy fingers.

My daughter and I stand on the footbridge
as I recall puffing my first cigarette
by this creek. I was just beginning
the second week of quitting.
I was planning to have
a funeral for my cigarettes.

I am so overcome by the fact
that the mothers of those girls died of cancer
before the girls finished high school,
which was a stylus of things to come
for Janet and Sharon.

I turn around and head back with the weight
of those four women tensed in every muscle
of my body. I lift my concrete feet slowly,
plod uphill as if the four women
were hunched on my shoulders.
I reach out for my daughter's hand.

Breaking Design

Hello My Name Is_____.
I'm from_____.

She reads the names of my hometown.
"That hellhole," she says.
We meet for the first time in thirty years.
Our last names, now different,
her thick glasses the same,
my blonde hair brown,
her brown hair gray.

"I was adopted by a family
thick in politics," she replies,
telling me her maiden name.

Oh, yes, in my class at school,
she disappeared abruptly
during our senior year.
She was the one
we all pushed aside
to get to someone else.

She still wears the Saint Christopher's
medal the English teacher gave
her the day she left.
But I know about leaving
and how you don't want
to look back, and how impossible it is
not to. How things play
over and over. How pain
is as new as the day it happened.

Her story entangled in mine.
The sunflowers have turned
their heads west.
There is a deep longing
to go home and confront,
but you can't.

Abandoned Homestead Protected by Farm Bureau

Mud pies with goldenrod,
sweet clover and milkweed
sun-baked in canning jar lids,
on the tar paper roof of a chicken coop.

Nailed into a mulberry furrow,
the rusted red and white sign reads
'Protected by Farm Bureau.'
Sounds from the tire swing circle,
awkward like hollyhock dolls.

Next to the summer kitchen,
tied to the pedal of a coarse grinder stone,
Zeke, the black chow, oversees.
Guaranteed imminent destiny,
a cloudy crystal ball.

The Advocate

He crosses a superhighway to kindergarten, shown only once by his father, after the move to Long Beach. He is a quick Mennonite boy with brown threshed hair, whose family sold out in Kansas, right down to the Rhode Island hens. Henry Maurice V never considers himself underprivileged.   It is expected that the five cents for a pint of milk in class be saved for his mother Lee Esther's treatment for melanoma.

Each night they would pack up to go to a treatment center in the drive-in movie theater. There Lee Esther would place her bare feet on a copper plate that was hooked up to wires producing current which they hoped would lead to a cure for melanoma . . . the year 1947, as the family of three watch a movie at the healing drive.

October 17, 1948 the Reverend who prayed with Lee Esther looks down the track at the train holding Lee Esther's coffin as it disappears into the distance beyond the vanishing point. Her husband, Henry Maurice IV, and five-year-old Mo are in the train that takes them back to Kansas.

They had missed the train earlier that morning due to smog. Later they learn that the train had derailed. Young Mo bawls like a wiggly calf while locked in the restroom, till the conductor removes the door.

II
Thirty years later that bawling calf on the train turned out to be my child's principal -- a child advocate. It was my youngest child. The last hand I had to hold. This five-year-old's first day of school.

The young straw-haired boy, nourished by Mo to play football in sixth grade, was allowed to bring Atwater the stray dog home on the school bus. It was Mo who reminded my son to put on long pants in February.

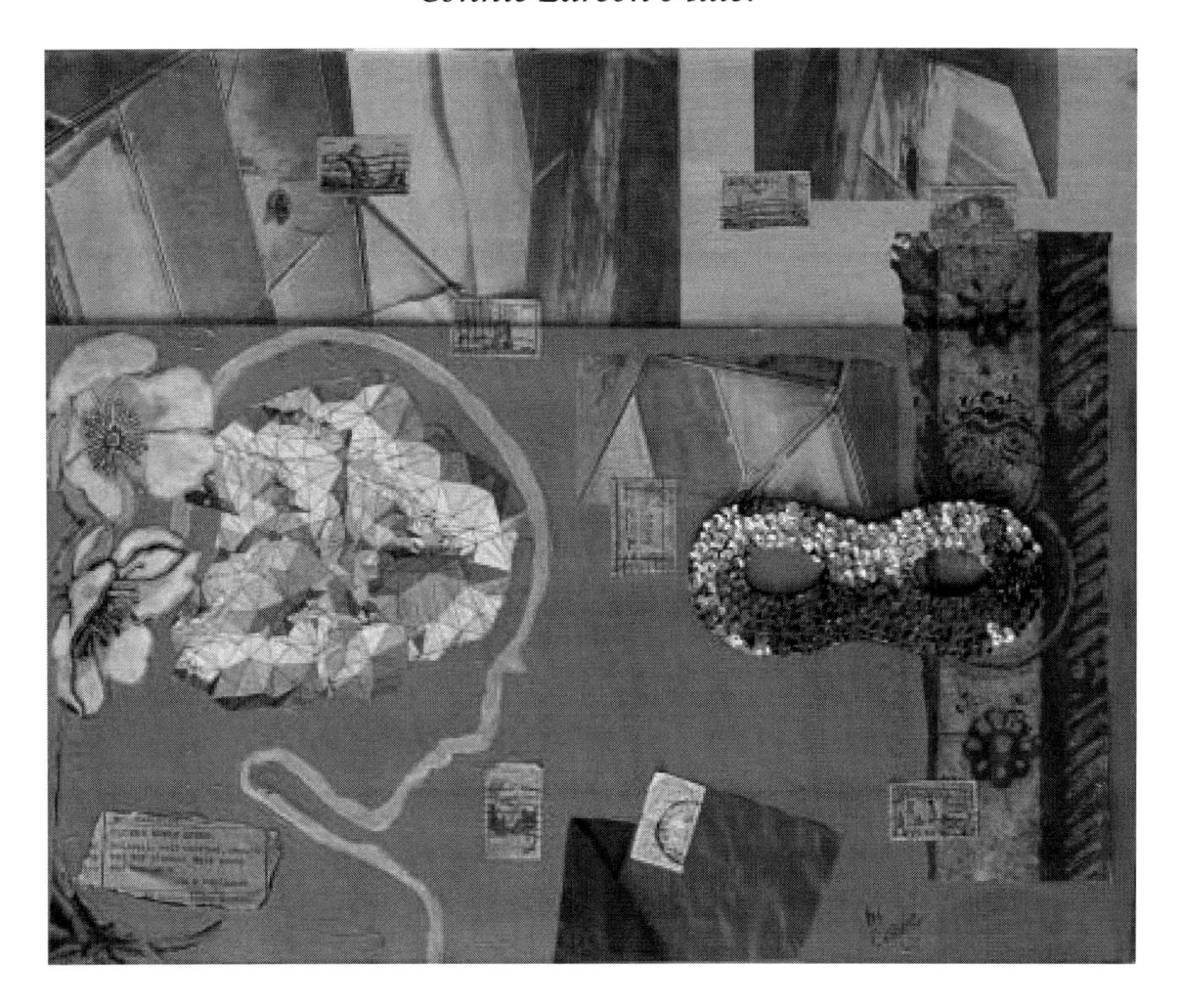

You see, this mother too had an illness and the treatment for mental illness was exploitation by the minister, and a doctor, and a banker husband in the sixties and seventies. Their traumatic ridicule suggests for mother that she should have an affair. So again, down the track to a distant land, the mother disappears to a vanishing point, to suffer in silence. She was too ashamed of the trio of their indignities to tell anyone what happened.

We all come to compassion at different times in our lives. For myself, I am grateful for what I have received.

Magical Powers

My memories of the keepsake red pencil
were made after climbing the stairs
to the platform at the ice plant.
Opening the door to my Dad's office,
the owners would be seated
on the chrome and maroon leather sofas,
smoking their Cuban cigars. Thumbs
in their vest pockets, they'd pull out
a penny and give it to me.

That's when I knew my Dad
had magical powers. Asking me,
"What color gumball do you want?"
He'd turn the gumball machine over
and sure enough,
there would be my red gumball!

I would proceed to play office
at an empty desk, with his pearl and red
Schaefer pencil, paper punch, stapler, and continue
swiveling from the Underwood
typewriter to adding machine.
I try to copy his efficiency --
something I still desperately try to imitate.

Memories of that lead pencil always
lying on the top of the chest of drawers
at night, ready to return
to his breast pocket for another day
of fastidious detail.

Connie Larson Miller

My father and the red pencil
could always get the right answers
to my trigonometry questions.
But he never could get the
calculation for the solution.

I recall the day he stopped making
me balance the checking account
to the penny by telling me to call
the bank and tell them they made
the mistake.

After you passed away, I opened the
utility door for the real estate lady.
All the dates of servicing were written
on each appliance and dated.
She simply said, "Your father was
wonderful with figures."

The night you died you held
up your hand with your imaginary
poker hand, announcing that I owed
you twenty-one cents. You said nothing
lasts forever and I reminded
you of what we'd been promised.
Whoever it was there with us,
yes, I'm sure they wanted you
to have the white suit.
You earned it.

Breaking Design

Just Things

The regulator clock is in my living room now.
Wound too tight, there is no chime.
No one to answer my questions or recall a forgotten name
as if the grapevine stem of the tree of life suddenly snapped.
The begonias you enjoyed last summer
are being cared for as you would have.
Even the Christmas cactus dares to bloom.
The initials I carved in grade school
in your antique chair, which now belongs to
my sister, are her intials too.
Your granddaughter wears the 50s dress
you made on your Singer sewing machine,
as if she had lived in the Donna Reed time frame.
And Lauren has your lucky goldpiece necklace.

Slowly, we find new homes for your things.
They were just old things to you.
I wanted to keep everything just as you left it.
It's me who wants to place myself up for adoption,
choosing you over and over again like a warped record
playing the same stanza.
That's what makes it so hard.

Catherine

She is the Godmother
who shines the narthex doors.
We learned to read music
by looking into her eyes.

Connie Larson Miller

Still Life with Missing Dog

Kites, eagles and hawks
whipsaw through the March air
with enough kite string
to see into the future.
I let the string out to the last inch,
tether, dive in and out of risk
afraid of the deep end,
of bobbing over my head.
Will you always look down on the lonely
old women whose children are grown?
Even the dog is gone.

I see myself as spoiled goods.
The splintered part stirs,
dumps itself in my lap,
clings to me like lint
when I rise each morning.
I try to brush it aside,
but it sits in my stomach
like unleavened bread.

Breaking Design

Prairie Chicken

I'm trying to explain what I'm doing here;
to a 'Midwestern' poet in Las Vegas
as she autographs my book, I say,
"I'm from the Midwest, too."
"Do you bake pie?" she asks.
"Should I ask do you have a pick ax?"

A drone at the drinking fountain asks,
"What do you do in Iowa?"
"Well, in the bars you can bet
on which numbered square
a caged chicken will shit on first."

Did I mention? "I love the four seasons?"
And in my backyard chickadees and red
squirrels chase from oak to elm.
My great grandfather Samuel homesteaded here.
It reminded him of the hills of Sweden.
I too, will be here with the Larsons, Andersons,
Burnsteds, Johnsons, disappear into the hills
beside Ida, Wilfred, Bertha and Reynold Carl.
Steal into the shadows of the red fox, coyote,
falcon, and prairie chicken.

I am marked with their touch
and the sound of the wind
over the grassy plain and a gravestone of soft lime,
where I first played hide and seek
with my cousins at midsummer in lantern light.
My father now takes his turn at the ice cream
freezer crank after adding more rock salt
and brushes sawdust off the ice,
then tops it with a quilt made from Samuel's
itchy wool suits he wore as the Commissioner

Connie Larson Miller

of the county seat. They bring out the long tables
from the basement and they are laid with fresh berry pies
and burnt sugar layer cakes, my favorite.

I cry for these, the faithful ones,
marked with the cross.
Here I am big with tenderness.

Breaking Design

At First She Only Flew When No One Looked
For Lydia

She sways on chocolate wedge mules
on a postage stamp dance floor,
as she snaps her fingers, nails platinum cherry jubilee.
Ornamental combs hold back a twist
of black ostrich wisps around the nape of her neck.
She draws out the rousing music of unforgotten years.
Soft obligato violin strings pull out the words
that would never come to me.

She sings truth as straight as a steel ray of sunrise.
She knows how to tell the evening sky
about the morning glories,
or tell us why the red-tailed hawk rises like soul,
or why cunning backroom boys shouldn't pass for wise.
And never question how sheep know their master's voice
or that grace is free.
Forever, I rake in her courage.

Albert

He pulls out his hearing aid
during coffee hour at church.
"Too much clatter," he says,
placing it in his overall breast pocket.
Says sometimes he hears things
he shouldn't, like couples talking dirty.
Other times he hears the angels.

Said his mama didn't want him to marry.
I guess some of those girls weren't too
nice at Number Nine School, suppose?
My mother always thought people
took advantage of Albert.
Gave him room and board,
wore his pencil down to a nub.

But today Albert is feeling just grand--
even heard the angels
as he has a sip of coffee,
half cream, and chews his dream
bar full of raisins and nutmeats.
Heaven's a little closer now.

Breaking Design

Milkweed Pods

During World War II things were rationed.
Grandpa Johnson saved a big ball of foil
made of gum and cigarette wrappers.

Milkweed pods were hoarded for the silky
substance inside the pods.
They were used to manufacture parachutes.

Dorothy worked as a parachute seamstress,
and when the war was over she and her fiancée wed.
She made her wedding dress from a parachute.

Sixty buoyant years later they came to worship
from Pennsylvania on a Sunday morning,
seeds of good will still afloat.

I recall this couple, how love
spills out so effortlessly.
Milkweed opening.

Mama Macaroni's Special Sauce

I'm the melted butter
that left you after the divorce.
The lump of flour is the knot
in my stomach that ached so I couldn't
see brown grass turn green.
My friend Margaret says
"You get better or bitter."
I've added both to the sauce.

When you come this Thanksgiving
bring all your seasoning,
your poster-thinness,
your dyslexia, your poverties
and your loneliness to add to mine
along with all our other talents
so we may savor each specialty,
spice and flavoring.

As we stir with our wooden spoons,
we dissolve each grain
of flour to give the melted butter form.
If it hadn't been for the hurts in the sauce
I could never have tasted
the rich thick bouillabaisse of seasoning
that life has to offer,
praising the blessings
even in my brokenness.

Breaking Design

On the Way to Minnesota

My sister and I count
red cars and black cows --
another game to keep us
from arguing over back
seat boundaries: twenty questions
animal, mineral and vegetable.
We all sang along
to "Name that Tune,"
until mother would say,
"Don't sing, Harold,
your voice is too gravelly,
and the children have
such sweet voices."
After that he was mute in church
and we all missed out.

At nightfall we sit
round the oilcloth-covered
table, listen to the night
sounds in our wool cardigans
and play Old Maid and Rook.
We were taught
not to care too much.

We drive all night back to Iowa.
I draw the short straw
and have to sleep in the well
of the back seat.
Thanks for the bumps,
Mom and Dad, but most of all
for second chances.

Rich Vein

I clutch fools gold on gravel
in front of the Johnson homestead,
as certain of its worth as the dust
on the row of peony bushes
along County Line Road.

I close my eyes, climb the worn stairwell,
find the door at the top painted turquoise
over scraped layers of coal smoked caramel,
the doorknob a cameo onyx.
When I knock she calls for me to enter,
sits in her rose brocade chair.

Grandma's persuasion of my character,
gentle as the sagging around her jowls,
upper arm to swollen ankles
puffing from her black tie shoes
and opaque oatmeal stockings.

Yet here I am in this church pew beyond
middle years. I turn to hear a jewel toned
child's voice sing out, "Here I Am, Lord."
Tears flow from my eyes, as if it's me singing.

Breaking Design

Baby with an Old Soul

Peach-pit-eyed shelter child
with your purple briar hair,
cheeks of autumn's hue.
Breakfast of Pop Tart
and gasoline soda pop baby bottle.
Trade apathy for gobbledygook
and beg me to pat-a-cake.
You look at me with wilted long face,
check the vantage point.
Dare me to peek-a-boo.
Walk up to the cannon's mouth
and let me waltz you up Rutledge Street, baby.

I too was old when I was young.
Add and subtract pounds to fury
my 32oz soda cup partner
to make life taste sweet.
Chased by yellow jacket
stings, a yo-yo wound tight.
I became suddenly serious,
lines furrow my forehead.

Shaylee

Shaylee's the last one at the collage
box, cinnamon hands churning
through pieces as unsatisfactory.
She throws it all aside like seconds
on a manufacturing line,
like an orphan in a soup line
looking for the only lifeline.

"Were you looking for shiny paper?"
"No," tossing her crocheted beaded cornrows.
"Do you like paper with hearts?"
She doesn't even look up.
"Was it a special piece?"
Her bedrock statement, "It was a card."

Then I recall the one greeting card
in box that had a black jazz trio on the front.

Shaylee sinks to undertow
and I feel as if I stepped on a landmine.
She snags the piece
and floats to her seat,
spirits buoyed.

Breaking Design

Connie Larson Miller

May 7, 1945

My father pores over Sunday's paper.
Sweat beads his brow
and mats his chest hair
around the oval cut of his undershirt.
But when I pull out
the chrome dinette chair
it clangs against a table leg.
I still hear its pierce.

My father puts down the paper,
commands I go outside,
get in the Plymouth
and honk the horn.
Without the slightest idea
how to interpret this,
I walk down the back stairs
to the car and make a tiny beep.
I return to the kitchen hoping to eat
without confrontation.

He stops me. "No,"
he says, "really honk it."
Puzzled, I go out
to the car and make a muffled beep.
But when I return
he's in the doorway
and comes down the backstairs,
bashes the screen door
wide with determination.
"Get back in the car
and really blast it."

Then he says, "I want you
to remember today, May 7, 1945.
The war's over."

Breaking Design

Cornflower Blue

Saw ole Jim Bob at the station yesterday.
Says he's "throwin' it in,
packin' up and moving to Shy Town.
Just can't take it no more."
Pond cracked clean like quartz,
couldn't skip a rock across it last spring.
Now just cattails and mud
peelin' up at the heels.

Everyone said great granddad Sven
was lonesome for the *old* country,
for choosin' that cowlick
homestead in the first place.
Now it's so dry, Ole said,
"just like murder in the hen
house stayin' around here."

Bertie Lindberg was poppin'
questions the other day
about what they did
with half cans of Bab-o.
She's been sizin' up her estate sale
for nearly twenty years.

Bet that granddaughter's
the last one to go.
Although she up and moved
to the county seat after tearin'
her hair out over that divorce.
Guess she up 'n' fell in love with tellin'
her grandmammy's story.
The dusty purple,
the faded sunlight,
the cornflower blue of it all.

The Year's Curve

I glance at crocus and hyacinths
along the curved brick path.
Peggy's yard was the pride of the neighborhood.
The flowers, her only love,
not enough to keep her from putting a gun
to her head that violent February.

It's been three years since the suicide attempt.
The gunshot only blinded her.
Passing her immaculately groomed yard,
now she scoots along the path
on a four-wheel platform. Pats the ground,
digs her finger in the soil to test the temperature.
She knows it's a clear creek-running day,
sounds of incredulous trickling, the first of April
and the sun shines on my neighbor's brick house.

All the sand from the ice storm
has been brushed aside.
As I tiptoe around the soggy parking, avoid puddles,
then repot geraniums left in the basement strung
with last fall's society page to caress them.
A handful of leaves from November
curl and trumpet on the sycamore branch
to once again make the royal announcement.

Spring.

Breaking Design

The December Earth Speaks

Tufts of Japanese Red Pine needles
scatter along the cold, gray sidewalk.
I pull my knit cap down to my collar,
listen as crisp, dry leaves scrape
and skid across my path.

Four arm-banded crows
circle a barren tree, stop and caw and keen
a cabaletta from the highest branch.
I avoid the scavengers
who look for a funeral director?

Night comes.
I toss in bed,
grip the comforter tight,
then bundle up
go out into the midnight air.

In the brilliant sky His light
shines down on me in Iowa,
you in Iraq, Italy, Iceland and Ireland.
Kissing me with starlight,
telling me, "Sing the song
of what I did for you on the tree."

Purple and turquoise
flip flops
with cha cha flower

Breaking Design

Eating Bitter Bread

How do I carry on after
a terrorist torching fire?
I commit more than ever
to convince a three-year-old
of a battered family
to break his entombment of the no's.

Coaxing, he abandons a protruding lip,
pushes a bunny cookie cutter through
the brown play dough,
and helps to pick up.

When I leave he says,
"no" to my good-bye.
It isn't no, don't leave.
but no I won't allow
you in my space.
He recoils into a stone
wall of defiance,
kicks the door
to the playroom closed.

No tireless hours of a fireman
battling for survivors.
Success for myself and this child,
I don't know.
What I do know is,
that for a moment,
this child and I forgot
our bitterness.

Newsreel

Abba, Abba, you sob
throwing your body
across a sand dune,
landing bended knee,
wailing for your father.
A stranger leads you away
by your forearm. Your sobs
are shown again and again.
They burn an image:
Suddenly you are the poster
child for Afghanistan.

I glance across my desk
at the picture of my great
nephew Parker, age five,
saluting in his father's
army fatigues.
Win or lose, some say,
we win by raising issues.
I commit to keep birds
in air, but my heart is heavy.

Breaking Design

The Women at the Well

They journey on the stony path
to the well at Galilee,
their steps repeated day after day,
lowering the bucket into the well
to bring up water.
Another day and another
they lower their bucket.
They do it so long that the well
is no longer a well.

It is the same with prayer.
Day after day we plead,
beg, ask for guidance,
praise and give thanks.
We ask forgiveness and blessing
year after year until prayer
is no longer the same.

It has become part of the well
from which we drew.
It has risen up and sprung from us.

Planing the Board

Jesus sizes up the board.
He turns it over, does the other side.
Shavings clutter the floor.

I have walked a terrible thin line.

Too much noise in my life.
Squawking ravens
warn each other.

My song changes as I walk.

The conductor listens
to us screech, practice as we play
our opus in harmony or discord.

Breaking Design

The Road That Brought Us Here
(Dorothea Lange's The Migrant Worker)

1.
I work the tired, tedious, rows
of seedless grapes. Pick
up gleanings for you,
my children, for your world.
You turn your face,
unwilling to share in the price.
"Home is what we know," you say.

2.
Tanks roll single file
across the tempered desert to Baghdad.
He bends double to build for you,
a maimed child, unable
to pick justice from the shards.

3.
We fly in dreams,
repeating as we fold and glide
our paper airplanes after school.
Gently we pry the borders of abuse
in the playroom of the crisis center.
Knowing the larger negative.

Jewelry Store Sky

Midnight trapeze
sparkling in jewelry store sky.
Held up by daybreak.

XX Chromosome

You no longer dictate.
I slip from golden
gingko into the winter,
see through
the imprisoning
venetian blinds.
Tail and headlights
flash,
ease forward.
Blinkers signal
intentions.

I appear,
am welcome
in the house of the Lord.
Kneel for supplication.
Chocolate shavings
on meringue.
A semi full of
drinking straws.

I used to think
hope was the most
important but
I misjudged.

Breaking Design

The Hard Part
*For 2nd Lieutenant
Michael Wade Smith*

You among the desert
date palm and poplar.
Sparse shade
to run to the beat
of a grinding tank
on Iraqi soil.
No longer able
to call home
somewhere near
the Euphrates.
Innocence explodes.

In return, I send
a box of red licorice
and hot tamales.
A lousy payment.

And I pray for the child
who longs to run
into your arms.
Waiting is the hard part.

Constructing a Paper Chain at the Crisis Center

Chartreuse, lemon and raspberry
   papers loop together,
gay as New York confetti.

Relationships rip apart.
   I patch, offer repair kits.
How do you spell unity for God's children?

I break, pull apart, and paste.
   It is not easy to erase
curses written in indelible red.

Breathe, yes, it does help
   to come up for air before
I get out the glue sticks again.

Connie Larson Miller

Loop Holes

School is canceled,
neighborhood children build a fort.
This is the day of no caffeine,
an orange leaf hanging on,
a day of enlightenment,
the muse audacity,
a day of the Mexican
blanket on the piano bench..

A rosy cheeked amaryllis is staked,
the blank page fills,
a day to polish cordovan shoes,
to lounge in a batik caftan.
A day of scarlet hibiscus tea,
a shadow across the room,
a day of cheese tortellini soup simmering.

This is a day to light
a candle for my nephew in Iraq,
a day to remember the faithful.
My cat Wadsworth attacks
the mother-in-law tongue.
It is the day of the belly dancer,
the poet, the weaver.

Breaking Design

Paisley Ghost Sighting II

Kira stews as she dresses.
Her homeroom readies
to be kangaroos.
Her mother made do
with worn out hand me downs
while other mothers shop
for witch brew grey or okra orange
for their children's costumes.

But guess what
Kira got to do?
Stand in the middle
as her costume
is pure character.
It was made from a flame-flowered
orange and avocado
drape from the living room.

"It's like a elephant with bamboo boots
or a bear in a Speedo," spews sister Maddie.

Syndey chimes in,
"That's nothing—once my brother
Jack was a Halloween ghost
in a pale paisley tablecloth."

Whew, doesn't that just give
you the heebie-jeebies?

Waiting for an Oil Change

The windowless waiting room
with its dust-covered schefflera,
plus stacks of magazines:
    Outdoor Life, Motor Age,
    Cattleman, and Gear.
I pretend to be curious about
fuel cells, but become conscious
of the fueling. I stand
still with gears unable to shift.
My joints too, need lubrication.

I blame it on these stale cigar-smoked
cinder blocks
needing air freshener,
sunlight and a dust cloth.

My feet began to twitch. My smile
is a slight bit higher on one side
of my mouth. My nose has a tic.
I walk down the street, buy
a treadmill, or was it a coat rack.

Breaking Design

At the Chat and Chew on Main

Coffee stains my blouse
and the beige and gold
speckled counter top.
Outside wind blows my hair,
sun's at my back,
and birds flirt down Main Street.

A pickup truck is parked on the west
side of the street.
A dog standing in the truck bed
settles down to wait.

Connie Larson Miller

A stray mongrel raises
his hind leg to the tire.

Two men in Big Smiths linger,
one lifts his cap to scratch his head,
they saunter into the Chat and Chew.
People who live here
know everybody else.

In the city building the election officials
squabble over the ninety-year-old janitor.
They decide because she needs the money,
they won't complain about how she does the job.

An unwaxed Dodge Dart
accelerates without a muffler.
A man walks by with his lunch purchase:
a plastic tub of Hormel spaghetti and meatballs.
You hear a rock click in the tire
of a flat bed truck loaded with cement blocks.

This is farming country
and once you're a farmer
you don't change.
You take an extra job
in the next town
but you don't quit farming.

I finish my day on the street
conducting an exit poll
in the Show-Me-State caucus.
A Lincoln pulls up with a wisp of lady
who clops in the city building
using a walker: drag-step, drag-step.

A jet stream streaks the distant sky,
a far off whistle blows,
and the doors of the grain
elevator roll closed.

The Breakfast Nook Story

In the year 1951, life was good. We had a console radio, and I had a Schwin bicycle, a dog and a three-speed phonograph, along with a vacant lot to play baseball. And when we had nothing else better to do, we'd take turns jumping off the front porch.

Our breakfast nook was located in our five-room brick bungalow and was accessible from the kitchen only. It was a small, out-of-the-way room, which contained a booth big enough for four people, a window seat, a cabinet, and the Coolerator. The Coolerator was known more commonly as an icebox. After school my friends and I would chip off slivers of ice with an ice pick from the ice block located in the top compartment, for our glasses of Kool-Aid. Most kids my age rather marveled at that. I hadn't given it much thought. I must admit I was always a little more experienced and could always chip off the largest or smallest bits with my skilled and trained hands. Life was good, simple and uncomplicated.

That was, until third grade. Our class was studying health, where words like *spoiling,* and *salmonella,* and the conveniences of modern refrigeration were mentioned -- things I really wasn't aware of. One day Mrs. Parkle, my teacher asked, "Is there anyone in the class who still has an icebox?"

For once, I was certain I knew the answer, so I quite proudly raised my hand and waved it back and forth—only, to my embarrassment, to find I was the only one with my hand up. My quick response had brought heads turning my way, and suddenly I found myself blurting out, "My father is the manager of Schafer Ice and Cold Storage."

To which Mrs. Parkle, rather in a gasping way, said sympathetically, "Well now, that explains it, doesn't it?"

Up until that time I hadn't remembered hearing my mother complain about throwing out spoiled food. But I began to notice her mentioning it. My mother added convincingly one night, "I don't see why we couldn't hide a refrigerator in the breakfast nook." My father's parents were part owners of the ice plant, and the thought of telling my grandfather that we would even consider buying a refrigerator sent my father shivering. "It would be like cutting off the hand that feeds you," he grumbled.

Preserving the family peace has always played an important part in my father's life. This time proved to be no exception, and soon after that, sure enough, we were hiding a brand-new refrigerator in our breakfast nook. Faithfully, to further ensure peace, my father continued to bring home a 25-pound block of ice -- which was taken out of the trunk of the car and left to melt in the garage -- just in case anyone would get suspicious at the ice plant, and hopefully covering up any evidence that we had succumbed to modern refrigeration.

It became the entire family's job to steer my grandparents away from the kitchen if they stopped by on a Sunday afternoon. Seems like years our family secret was kept. At family dinners, the grandparents were not to do dishes or even carry their plates to the kitchen, which usually meant more work for me.

Then years later, my father decided to casually mention it to his parents. "Well, Helen and I," he fumbled. "well, we're thinking of getting a refrigerator." I think it even surprised him that he told his parents.

"About time, I'd say," he added agreeably like he'd been waiting for years to hear that. Soon after that my grandparents purchased a new gold Frigidaire with lazy-Susan shelves.

Breaking Design

Midnight stars
sparkling in jewelry store sky,
heldup by daybreak.

Connie

Connie Larson Miller

Lady with a Lathe

Sharon's mother married at fifteen.
Sixty years later she's still married
to the same guy who survived cancer
after a partial lung was removed.
He tried to go back to work, but
found his job replaced by a computer.
His children pitched in to buy him
his second life: a lathe.

Sharon and I met on a shuttle
to a workshop at Arrowmount
School of Arts and Crafts.
Now she works on her second life
after cancer surgery
and breast reconstruction
from a muscle in her back.

Her hair is streaked tigers eye
which she clasps straight back.
As Friday night comes she forms
a drinking vessel with water and chisel
and lets the chips lie as I shape
doormat passions into journals.
I, too, join in the line for her back massage
as we wait for a visiting lecturer.

Saturday on the way through
the narrow spun road of the Smokies,
she smells of hardwood maple.
She makes a plan to turn a bat
for her slugger grandson's
birthday at home in Dallas.

I stand back and admire --
clutch my demons to my chest.

Breaking Design

Smug Sydney

Smug Sydney in
calico kerchief reflects in Daddy's
mirrored sunglasses

Driving Good Gifts into Hiding

There is a place along the river
where he commands the cottonwoods
silent. But he couldn't keep them
from whispering.

Just as he plowed out prairie,
we woke to the want
of milkweed and falcon.

I pull cornhusks from my sleeves
along the interstate
spreading from town
into greedy blacktop.
And he snatches a dime
from the pig lot.

And then there was a woman
who offered up her suffering
so that her children
would have faith.

The poor have such a luxury.

Cardinal

Admiral of birds
stays on in February
to flash me his
siren red from flight
to juniper branch

My heart stops
its throb to see the nest
in the cherry tree.

Breaking Design

Sunday Is In Me Now

The ice storm passes.
Midnight starlight bright
as Monday's washday.
Tree branches fall,
crinkle like sterling silver teaspoons
on wind chimes.
Tomorrow the heads of households
are their brother's keepers
with competing snow blowers.
Stocking caps covering their ears,
eyes water down their chapped cheeks.

Flashing yellow,
unfrozen feelings thawing,
proceed with caution.
A cup thrown on the floor
made new, by selling
on eBay for profit.

What can I do to atone for February?
Write red licorice laced Valentines
And chew cinnamon gumdrops?
Love is a glad surviving heart.

My Father's winter chore ---
gluing rocket-shaped deer whistles
back on our bumpers
from the carwash.
A dear himself.

Night-Time Blessings

Bless Polly for putting the kettle on.
Bless the little blue engine who thought he could.
Bless the gingerbread man who ran and ran.
And bless the tortoise who won the race.
Bless the mice with their tails cut off.
And don't forget the stones in the soup.
Bless the hen that bakes the bread
And the old women whispering hush.
Bless the church and the church steeple
and especially bless all the people.
Bless the stories yet to be told
and bless the ones we know.

Breaking Design

Closing

We look into the eyes
of the Virgin Mary -- ask
to have the heart of Jesus.
The thrill of the dove's soft coo
in the morning in our ears.
The taste of the bread
of hospitality, the sun
shining on the page we script.
The sway of the branches directs us.
We praise the light and the shadow,
smooth and rough, thick and thin,
the thirst and the fullness,
the sorrow and the joy.
We are at this place
because at this moment,
in this minute, in this hour,
this is where we are supposed to be.
We are blessed and to you
we say yes, God.

Connie Larson Miller lives in southeast Iowa, where she grew up. She is the mother of three grown children. Soon to have her fifth grandchild, she is known lovingly as "Grandma, No, No" to them and as "Rockin' Grandma" to the children of the local Crisis Center, where she volunteers. She works with VSA arts of Iowa to teach visual arts, poetry and storytelling across the state. Connie has an AA degree from Indian Hills Community College, and she thrives on taking workshops and retreats. *Breaking Design* is her first book, although her poetry has been widely published in magazines and journals.

Other books from PBL Limited

publishing and book distribution

Focus on Photos $24.99
Mars Hill – A Living Legacy $24.99
St. Patrick's Georgetown $24.99
Concerning Mary Ann $26.99
Items from the Bluegrass $19.99
JANET! $19.99
Meet Me At the Fair $19.99
"Come, Let Us Journey" $19.99
Pilgrimage $19.99
St. Joseph Hospital $19.99
Ottumwa $19.99
Ottumwa Postcards $19.99
Inklings $19.99
The Narrow Gate $19.99
Days Gone By $19.99
Coming Up Dry $19.99

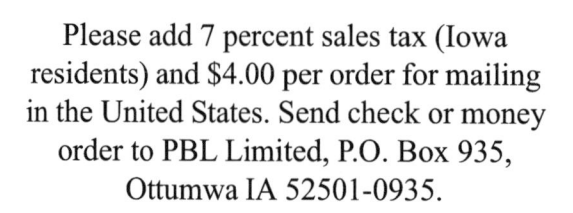

Visit our website at www.pbllimited.com to view these and other titles.

Please add 7 percent sales tax (Iowa residents) and $4.00 per order for mailing in the United States. Send check or money order to PBL Limited, P.O. Box 935, Ottumwa IA 52501-0935.